GOLF
is for me

Mark Lerner

photographs by
Robert L. Wolfe

Lerner Publications Company   Minneapolis

The author would like to thank Jeff Bland, Phil Hurrle, Kelli Ross, Sarah Elton, and Dick Hannah for their help with this book. A special thanks is given to Jim Werre, pro at Braemar Golf Course, Edina, Minnesota.

To Dad, the expert putter

LIBRARY OF CONGRESS CATALOGING IN PUBLICATION DATA

Lerner, Mark.
   Golf is for me.

   (A Sports for me book)
   SUMMARY: Follows a young boy as he learns the fundamentals of golf from a local pro and plays a round with three other beginners.
   1. Golf—Juvenile literature. [1. Golf]
I. Wolfe, Robert L, ill. II. Title. III. Series: Sports for me books.
GV965.L495   796.352   81-20927
ISBN 0-8225-1143-6   AACR2

Copyright © 1982 by Lerner Publications Company

All rights reserved. International copyright secured. No part of this book may be reproduced in any form whatsoever without permission in writing from the publisher except for the inclusion of brief quotations in an acknowledged review.

Manufactured in the United States of America

International Standard Book Number: 0-8225-1143-6
Library of Congress Catalog Card Number: 81-20927

Given in Memory of
Wilton H. Talley and Elizabeth A. Talley
by Julia Talley Draucker

Hi. I'm Jeff, and I like to play golf. My sister Laura plays golf for her high school team. Watching Laura play made me want to try golf, too.

In golf, you use clubs to hit a small ball into a hole. Most golf courses have 18 holes, but some, especially those for younger players, have only 9 holes. Each time you hit the ball, it is counted as a **stroke**. You try to take as few strokes as possible to sink your ball into the holes. At the end of a match, the golfer with the lowest number of strokes is the winner.

One day after school, I went to the golf course with Laura. At the course, I saw a sign announcing golf lessons for people my age. Laura thought I'd enjoy learning golf, so she suggested that I take lessons.

I signed up for lessons in the **pro shop**. In the pro shop, golfers can buy equipment and rent clubs to play with if they don't have clubs of their own.

My first lesson was the following week. I went to the golf course and was introduced to Jim, the golf **pro.** Golf pros are experienced golfers who teach people how to play or how to improve their game. Pros teach both children and adults.

First Jim showed me the equipment used in golf. He said most beginning golfers should start out with seven golf **clubs**: two **woods**, four **irons**, and one **putter.** Jim set these clubs on a golf bag for me and said I would have to practice a lot to use all of the clubs well.

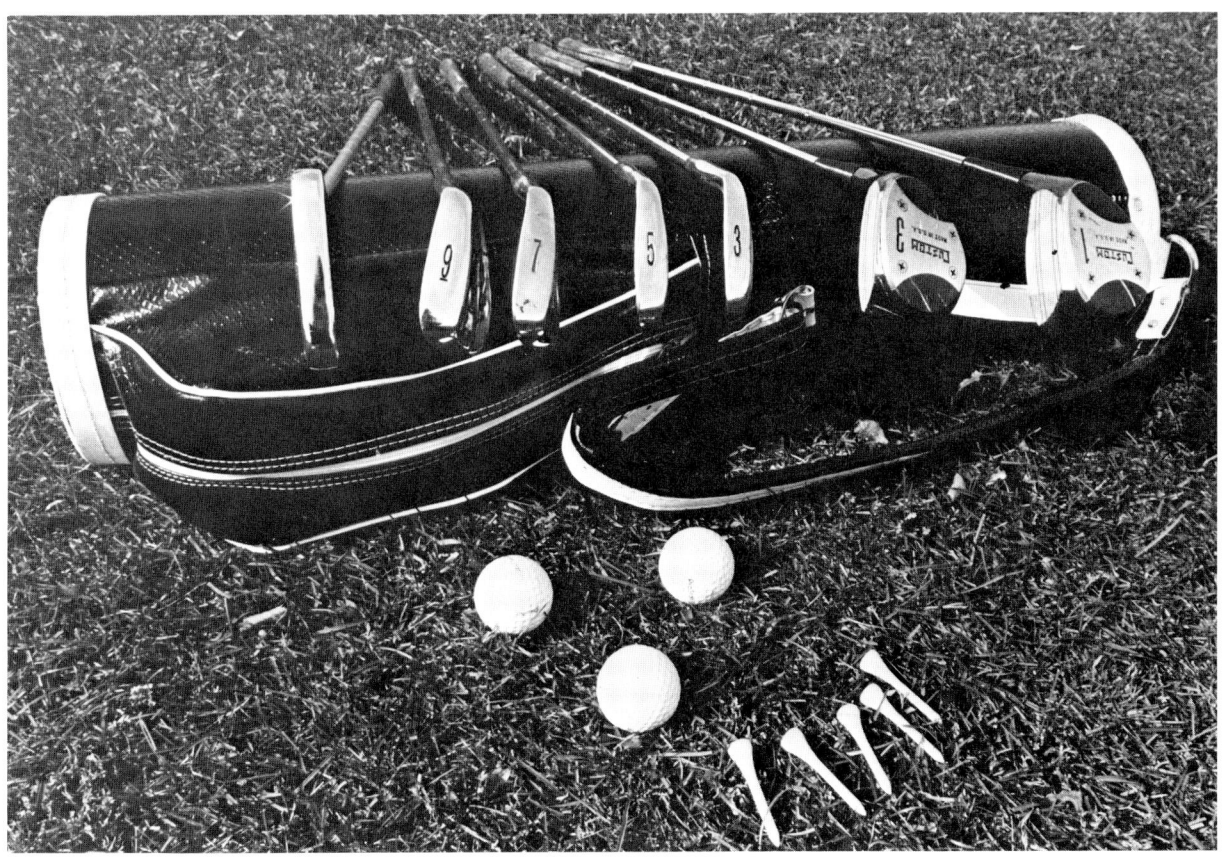

Jim said that before I could use a club, I had to learn how to hold it properly. The **grip,** or the way you hold the club, is very important in golf.

Jim said young golfers should grip the golf club like a baseball bat. If you're right-handed, place your left hand just below the cap on the top of the club's **shaft.** The shaft is the long part of the club.

The shaft is attached to the **club face,** the part of the club you hit the ball with.

Your left thumb should point directly down the shaft, and your fingers should be wrapped lightly around it. Then put your right hand on the club next to the left hand. The little finger on your right hand should touch the left index finger. This is called the **baseball grip.**

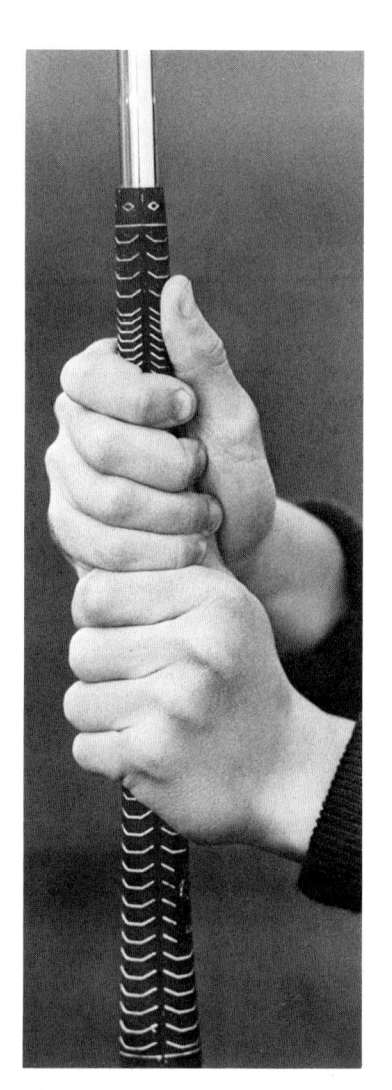

In golf, getting ready to hit the ball is called the **address**. You must put your feet in the right place, extend your arms and the club, and keep your back straight.

Jim taught me the address routine by setting three clubs on the ground. Each club represented a line that golfers should remember before hitting a shot. The first line is the **target line**.

The target line is the path you want your ball to take on its way to the hole, or target.

Then Jim showed me the **ball line**. That's the short imaginary line between the ball and your feet. If you're a right-handed golfer, the ball line goes from the ball to your left heel. Your left foot should be slightly turned and pointed toward the target.

The third club was meant to show the **foot line**. Jim put that club parallel to the target line. The foot line is the imaginary line you must keep your feet behind.

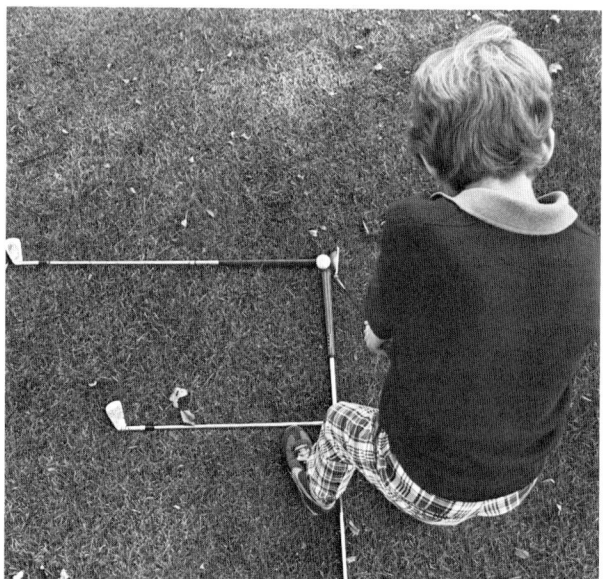

The clubs on the ground gave me a good idea of how and where I should stand for the address routine. During a real golf game, the clubs won't be on the ground in front of me. But for practicing the correct **stance**, or way to stand at the ball, they're a big help.

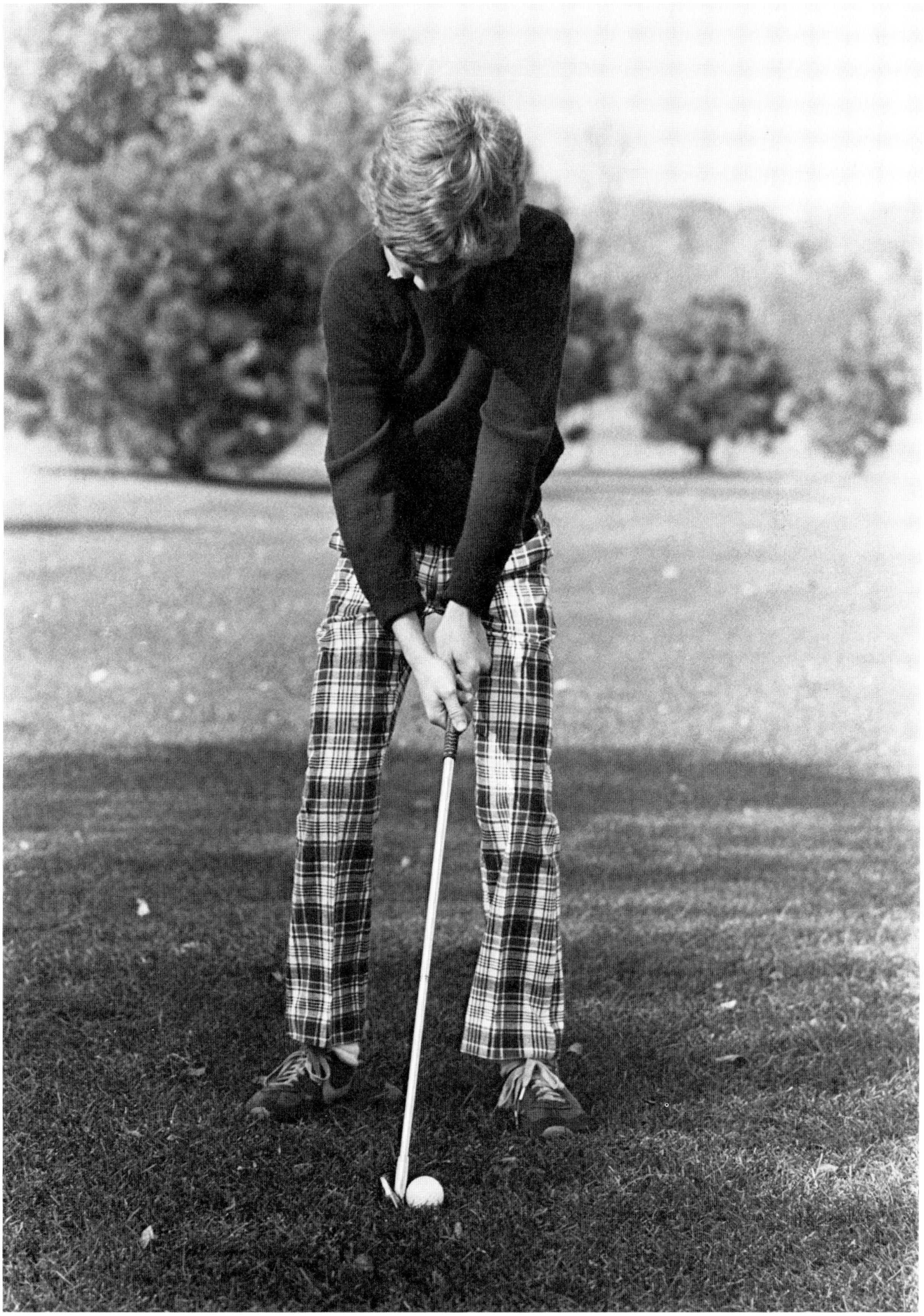

Now that I had learned the grip and stance, Jim said it was time to try my swing. The first thing to remember about the swing is that your hands, arms, and shoulders should form an upside-down triangle.

Another thing to think of while you swing is an imaginary **hub,** or point, on your chest. Try to think of the hub as the center of a clock, and your club as one of the clock's hands. When you swing, your club should move completely around the hub in one motion.

Jim said that the first part of the swing is called the **takeaway.** That's when you bring your club back behind you and over your head.

During the swing, always remember to keep your head steady and to keep your eye on the ball. Even after you hit the ball, your head should stay down, and you should look at the spot where the ball was.

By practicing that, you'll learn to keep your head in the right place every time you swing.

The last thing Jim told me about the swing was to swing *through* the ball to finish the shot. Don't stop swinging after you've hit the ball. Keep the swing going until you've swung your club well out in front of you.

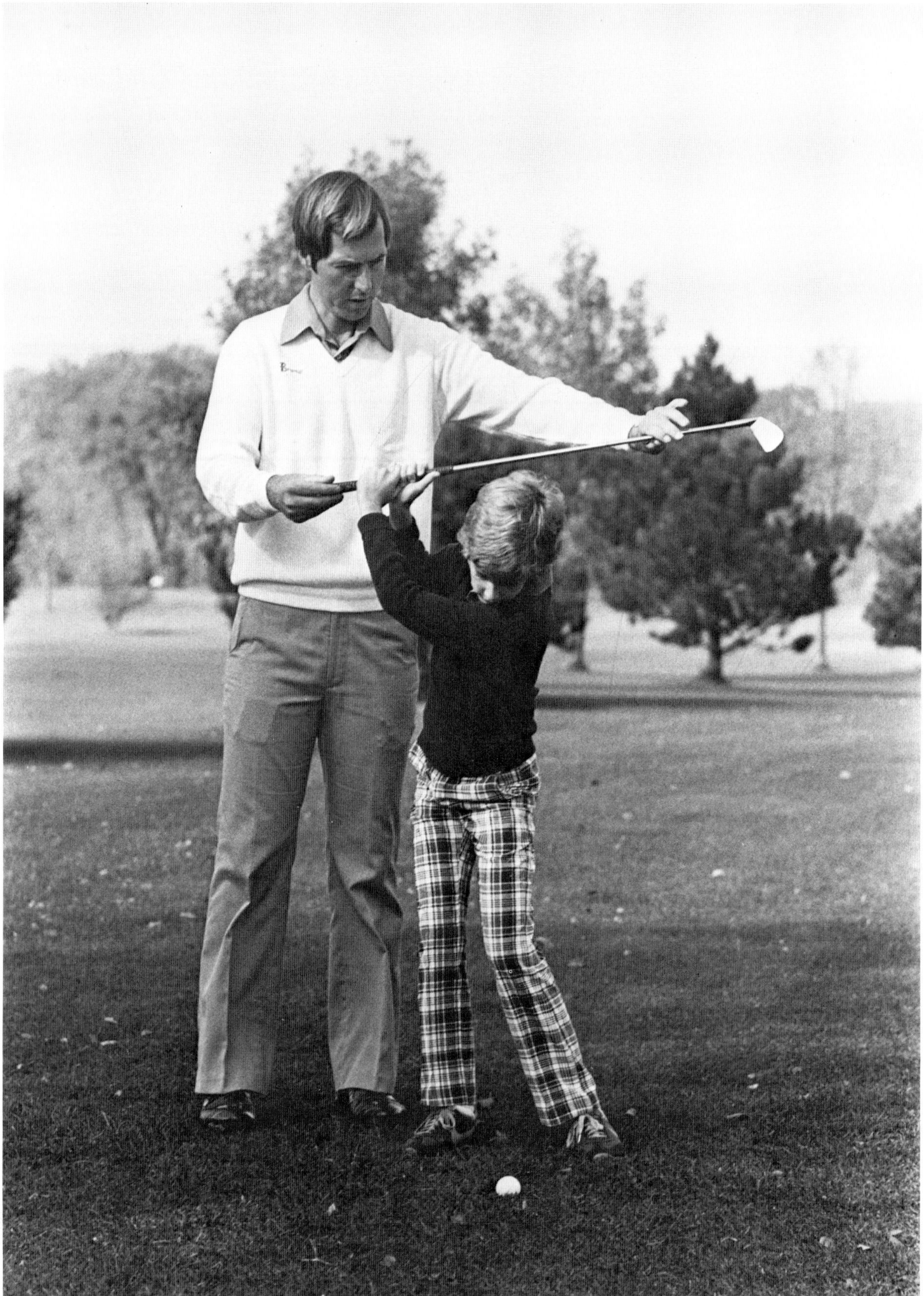

At first, everything that Jim told me seemed like a lot to remember. But after I had practiced swinging a few times, everything went well. The balls I hit didn't go very far, and they weren't very high off the ground. But I did hit them, and that made me feel good.

When it was time to go home, Jim told me to go over in my mind everything I had learned in my first lesson. Jim said that golf requires thinking as well as action. So it's a good idea to think about your game even when you're not on the golf course.

The next week, Jim started my second lesson by explaining the **approach.** You use an approach shot after your **tee shot.** The tee shot is the first shot for each hole as you try to reach the **green.** The green is the area around the hole. If you make a good approach shot, your ball will land on the green and maybe very close to the hole.

Jim said that short approach shots are also called **chip shots**. You use your irons to hit chip shots. Experienced golfers may have up to 10 different irons, but Jim said that beginners should start with four: the 3, the 5, the 7, and the 9.

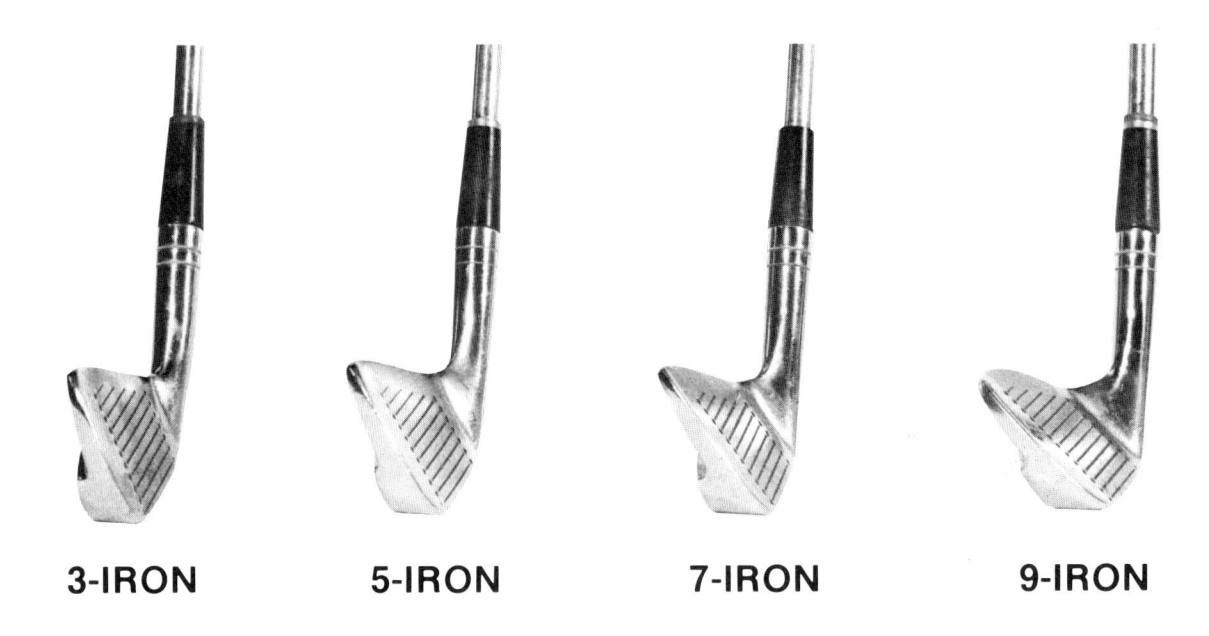

3-IRON   **5-IRON**   **7-IRON**   **9-IRON**

Each club has a slightly different **face**. The face is the angle the club is turned. Irons with high numbers, like 7, 8, and 9, have club faces with a greater **loft,** or backward slant, to them. Golfers use the high-numbered irons when they are close to the green, and low-numbered irons when they are far away from it.

Now I was ready to try the different irons. To start, Jim told me to shorten my grip on the shaft of the club. So I put my hands farther down on the club than I did when I hit a tee shot. Jim also told me to widen, or open up, my stance.

When chipping, bend your body to get closer to the ball. You form a triangle as you do when you are hitting any shot.

I practiced the grip and stance. Then Jim showed me the swing that golfers use for chip shots. Jim said your swing should change for chip shots of different distances.

For a **lower running shot**, bring the club back to a spot just below your knees. Lower running shots are supposed to go a long distance, so you want the ball to roll towards the hole after it hits the ground. For lower running shots, use a low-numbered iron, like the 5 or the 7.

The **higher lofting shot** is another kind of chip shot. You should use a higher lofting shot when you want the ball to travel over something. On your swing for a higher lofting shot, bring the club back to a spot a few inches above your knees and use an 8-iron or a 9-iron.

Jim said it would take time for me to know exactly how far to bring the club back for each chip shot. But with practice I would find the right swing for each shot.

All golfers hit balls into **sand traps** now and then. So another shot I learned was the chip shot from sand. Jim said learning how to hit out of traps is not difficult but very important to know. I was surprised when Jim said that you don't actually need to hit the ball to knock a ball out of the sand. Instead, you hit the sand *behind* the ball and make an **explosion shot**.

For an explosion shot, take a full swing with your 9-iron and try to hit the sand an inch or two behind the ball with as much force as you can. Then follow through as usual. The sand you've hit will power the ball out of the sand trap. I tried a few sand shots and did pretty well. Sand traps are not fun to get into, but they're a challenge to get out of.

In the next part of the lesson, Jim showed me how to **putt.** In order to be a good golfer, you have to be a good putter. And to be a good putter, you have to know how to **read the green.** Greens curve in different ways, and it takes much practice to learn how to **read,** or play, them right.

Sometimes you must putt uphill and sometimes downhill. Or you might have to putt at an angle. When you putt at an angle, you don't aim straight for the hole. Instead you aim according to how you think the ball will **break,** or curve, toward the hole.

Before you putt, crouch behind the ball and try to imagine how the ball will travel on its way to the hole. When you're behind the ball reading the green, you should think about how hard or how gently you will need to hit the ball. You'll also want to think about the **contour** of the green, or how flat or hilly it is. And if the green is wet, you must think about that, too. Balls break more slowly on wet greens than on dry ones.

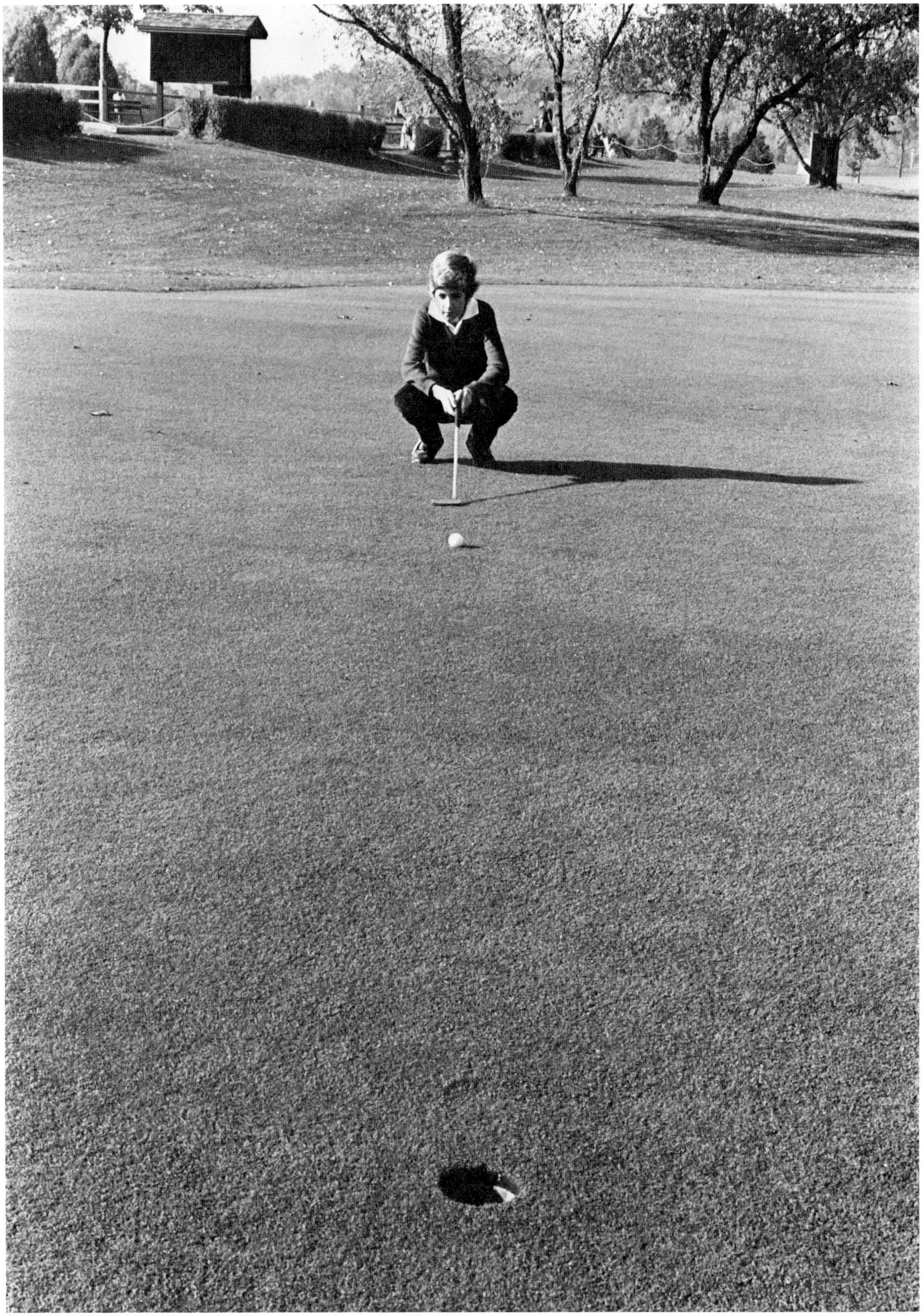

Reading the green right is only the first step of a good putt. Next you must hit the ball just right. Jim showed me the putting stance and said that your eyes should be directly over the ball. Your weight should be balanced equally on each leg with the ball centered between your feet and a few inches away from them.

Jim said the putting swing is actually just a short, smooth stroke. Bend over the ball and bring the club about one foot straight back. Then firmly but lightly stroke the ball. Keep the lower part of your body motionless and your putter close to the grass.

I practiced a few putts. I know it will take a while to learn how to play all the little hills and valleys on the greens.

On our way back to the pro shop, Jim and I stopped at the **driving range**. Some grown-ups were hitting **drives** with their woods. Jim said I should try some drives, too. I took out my 1-wood, the longest club in my golf bag. Jim said that the woods are the toughest clubs to use. They are long, and they don't have much loft.

23

I pushed a **tee** into the ground. A tee is a small wooden peg that you stick into the ground and set your ball on before hitting a drive. I put the ball on the tee and got into my regular stance. Jim told me to take a full swing like I had done when I learned the swing at my first lesson.

At first my drives didn't go very far. But then I hit some good ones. I liked driving. It was easy to see why some golfers came to the golf course just to practice their drives on the driving range. It's exciting to see your ball fly through the air and land a long distance away.

Driving was the last part of my lesson. Before I went home, though, Jim had a surprise for me. He said that for my next lesson I would play a nine-hole match with three other young golfers he was teaching. We would have a **foursome** and compete against each other. I was going to play in my first golf match!

All I could think about during the week was golf. When Saturday finally came, I went to the course early. Jim was there, and he told me the other golfers would arrive soon. Jim and I waited in the pro shop, and I rented my set of clubs for the day. It wasn't long before Kelli, Sarah, and Phil arrived. They were all as excited to play in a foursome as I was.

Before we started the match, Jim said we should loosen up. Each of us took some practice swings and stretched our muscles a bit. The first hole was 112 yards long, **par 3.** That means the hole was 112 yards from the tee, and the average golfer should use only three **strokes,** or shots, to sink the ball into the hole. Making par would be tough for us because we weren't experienced golfers.

Kelli teed off first. On her first swing she **whiffed,** or missed the ball completely. Whenever you try to hit the ball, it's counted as a stroke, even if you miss. Whiffs count as strokes, so we had to count one stroke against Kelli. Kelli hit the ball on her second swing, but it didn't go very far. I think she was pretty nervous.

Sarah was next, and she hit a good drive. It soared high and long, and it landed to the left of the green. Sarah's shot would be tough to top.

I decided to use a 3-iron on my tee shot because Jim said a wood might make me drive the ball too far. I drove the ball about 80 yards. That was a pretty good first shot.

Phil went next and his ball landed in some thick grass around a bunch of leaves.

After all four of us had hit our first shots, we walked down the **fairway** to get ready for our second shots. The fairway is the playing area from the tee to the green. Phil was the farthest from the hole, so he was first to take his second shot. It was a hard shot because his ball was in tall grass, but he used a 9-iron and hit a good shot. His ball landed on the green, only two feet from the hole.

Kelli was next. She hit the ball really well, but it went too far and over the green and almost into the water. On my shot, I made it to the green, but just barely. Sarah's second shot wasn't very good. It landed in the sand.

With Kelli's ball so close to the water, she had a difficult third shot to make. But she hit a good one, and her ball landed on the green. Since she was in the sand, Sarah also had a tough shot. After she hit her shot, she raked the sand trap. Explosion shots from the traps make the sand fly.

So as a courtesy to other golfers, you should smooth out the sand trap with a rake after you've hit out of it.

Sarah's shot from the sand landed on the green, and that made her happy. She had made a good **recovery**. You make a recovery whenever you hit a good shot from a bad position like a sand trap. Now we were all on the green, ready for putting.

My putt didn't break the way I thought it would. The green was wet from rain the night before. I had forgotten about that when I putted, and I missed the hole by inches. Because I was so close, I tapped the ball in without waiting for my turn to come up again. When you're very close to the hole, it's best to finish up and get your ball out of the way of other players' shots.

I shot a four on the first hole. That was one stroke over par. Shooting one stroke over par is called a **bogey**. A **double-bogey** is two strokes over par. Unfortunately, Kelli double bogeyed. The long putt on her fourth shot just missed the hole. She didn't sink the putt until her fifth shot.

Phil, though, made his par on the first hole. He sank the ball on his third shot. Sarah finished the first hole in four strokes, so she and I were tied. Sarah was keeping score on our scorecard. Here's what our scores were at the end of hole number one:

On the second hole, each of us got into trouble. Phil shot first because he had had the lowest score on the hole before. His ball went straight into the woods. We all went to look for it, and Phil finally found it.

On my turn, I hit into the woods, too. We all went ball hunting again, but nobody could find it. If you don't find your ball in five minutes, you are **penalized** two strokes.

Because of the penalty, I had two strokes against me after only one shot. Phil used a 7-iron on his second stroke. He hit a nice shot from the woods, and his ball made it to the green. Sarah and Kelli didn't hit very good shots, but at least neither of theirs landed in the woods!

My ball was lost, so I had to put a new one into play. I reshot from the tee, and I hit the ball too far. It rolled right over the green.

Kelli had hit her ball on a slope, so on her third shot she had to aim to the left. She did that, and she made it to the green. On her fourth stroke, she almost sank a very long putt. Now she only had to tap the ball in. Before she putted, though, she cleaned a leaf off her ball.

Golfers are allowed to clean their balls if they're dirty. You put a marker on the ground where your ball was. Then you clean off the ball and replace the marker with your clean ball.

When it was Phil's turn, he measured his putt carefully. He crouched and looked at the green and took a long time to line up the putt. He sank the putt from about 12 feet out.

After the second hole, Phil was winning the match. He had a score of 8. Sarah had 9. And Kelli and I each had 10.

For the next five holes, the match was very close. On one hole, Kelli had a **birdie**. A birdie is one stroke under par. Kelli sank her ball in two strokes on a par-3 hole.

When we got to the eighth hole, Phil was the leader with a 45, and Kelli had a 46. I had 49, and Sarah had 50. Hole number eight was the shortest on the course—only 71 yards—but it had a **water hazard**. You had to hit your ball over a small pond. There was no way to get around it.

Phil went first. He hit the ball easily over the water. So did Kelli. But I wasn't as lucky. On my swing I hit too much **turf**, or grass, and not enough of the ball. A **divot** flew up from under my club as my ball plunked into the water. A divot is a piece of turf that golfers dig up when hitting the ball.

I had to put a new ball in play just behind the water. I hit the new ball with a 7-iron and landed the ball on the green.

Now we were down to the last hole, number 9. Phil was still ahead with a 49, and Kelli had 50. Sarah and I were tied at 54. The ninth was going to be a tough hole to play.

Phil hit first, and his ball rolled behind a tree on the fairway. He had a **stymie**. That's when you can't hit the ball forward toward the green. Instead you have to hit the ball sideways, back to the clear part of the fairway.

Kelli made a great tee shot. Using her wood, she hit the ball over the tree that Phil's ball was behind and landed her ball on the green about 15 feet from the cup. Sarah got to the green in two strokes, and so did I. We were close to the cup, so we tapped in. Sarah and I each finished the ninth hole with fours.

Phil, though, was having a hard time. He had to recover from his stymie, and that took an extra stroke. He didn't make it to the green until his third stroke.

Phil putted on his fourth stroke. His ball rolled around the **lip**, or sides, of the cup, and then it fell in. He bogeyed, as Sarah and I had.

Now it was Kelli's turn. If she made her 15-foot putt, she would birdie and win the match. Kelli took her time lining up the putt. She knew she had to think about the wet green and its slight downward slope. I stood behind the flag, ready to pull it up out of the hole before the ball rolled in.

44

Kelli putted and the ball broke perfectly for her. When the ball was about two feet away, I pulled the flag from the cup and watched. The ball rolled in. Kelli had made it! She had a 52 for nine holes, one stroke better than Phil. Kelli had won. Sarah and I each had 58, so we tied for third place.

Jim congratulated us all on a fine match. We had a lot of fun, and Jim said we had all played very well. He told us that the more we played, the better we would become. And that's just what I will do. I know that golf is for me!

Words about GOLF

ADDRESS ROUTINE: The way golfers position their feet, arms, shoulders, and backs when getting ready to swing

APPROACH: The shots taken to get the ball down the fairway

BALL LINE: The short imaginary line between the ball and the player's feet

BASEBALL GRIP: A way of holding the club with the little finger on one hand touching the index finger of the other, like gripping a baseball bat

BIRDIE: A score one stroke under par on a hole; for example, shooting a 2 on a par-3 hole

BOGEY: A score one stroke over par on a hole; for example, shooting a 4 on a par-3 hole

BREAK: The slope or curve of a green

CHIP SHOT: The shot golfers take in their approach to the green

CLUBS: The woods, irons, and putter golfers use to hit the ball

CLUB FACE: The bottom part of the club with which golfers hit the ball

DIVOT: A piece of turf, or grass, that golfers dig up when hitting the ball

DOUBLE-BOGEY: A score two strokes over par on a hole; for example, shooting a 5 on a par-3 hole

DRIVE: The first shot taken from the tee

DRIVING RANGE: An area where golfers practice hitting the ball

EXPLOSION SHOT: A shot from a sand trap. The sand behind the ball is hit, causing the sand and the ball to explode from the trap at the same time.

FAIRWAY: The grassy area between the tee and the putting green

FOOT LINE: The imaginary line golfers must keep their feet behind for balance and a good swing

GREEN: The smooth area surrounding the hole, or cup. Also called the putting green.

GRIP: The way golfers hold the club

HIGHER LOFTING SHOT: A chip shot golfers use when they are close to the green

HUB: An imaginary point on the chest around which a golfer should swing the club

IRONS: The clubs used for the approach to the green

LOFT: The backward slant of a club face. The higher the number of a club, the greater its loft.

LOWER RUNNING SHOT: A chip shot golfers hit to make the ball travel a long way and roll after it hits the ground

PAR: The average number of strokes a golfer should take to sink the ball into the hole. On a par-3 hole, for example, a golfer should take only three strokes to sink the ball.

PRO: An experienced golfer who teaches the game to beginners or to other golfers

PRO SHOP: The place at a golf course where golfers may buy or rent equipment

PUTTER: The club used for hitting the ball into the hole

READ THE GREEN: To decide how hard and at which angle to putt the ball into the hole

RECOVERY: A good shot from a bad position such as a sand trap

SHAFT: The long part of the club. Golfers grip the club near the top of the shaft.

STANCE: The way golfers stand at the ball before hitting it

STROKE: One shot in golf; hitting the ball with the club

STYMIE: When a tree or other obstacle gets in the way of the ball. The golfer cannot hit the ball forward, only backward or to one side.

TAKEAWAY: The first part of the swing, when the club is brought behind and over the golfer's head

TARGET LINE: The path golfers want the ball to take on its way to the hole

TEE: A small wooden peg which holds the ball in place for a tee shot

TEE SHOT: The first shot at each hole

WATER HAZARD: A pond or stream over which a golfer must hit the ball. Golfers whose balls land in the water get a one-stroke penalty.

WHIFF: To swing at the ball but miss it completely

WOODS: The largest golf clubs, used to hit the ball long distances